31 DAY
DEVOTIONAL

Prophetess Tera Person

Victory For The Day 31 Day Devotional
Copyright © 2024 Tera Person

For bookings for a preached word or motivational speaking
contact Prophetess Tera Person at:
terapersoninternationalministries@gmail.com

 Also check out the YouTube channel:
Prophetess Tera Person International Ministries

Book Completion Services Provided by:
TRU Statement Publications—Independent Publishing Made Easy
www.trustatementpublications.com

First Edition: August 2024
Printed in the United States of America
All Rights Reserved
0 0 8 0 2 0 2 0 2 4 0 0
ISBN: 9798334852891

31 DAY
DEVOTIONAL

Prophetess Tera Person

How to Use This Devotional

Welcome to "Victory for the Day: 31 Day Devotional!" This devotional is designed to guide you on a daily journey of faith, perseverance, and victory. Each day's entry includes a scripture, a devotional message, a reflection question, and a decree statement to help you meditate on God's promises and strengthen your faith.

Steps to Make the Most of This Devotional:

1. **Find a Quiet Space**: Begin by finding a quiet place where you can spend uninterrupted time with God. This will help you focus and connect deeply with the day's message.

2. **Read the Scripture**: Start each day by reading the scripture provided. Take a moment to reflect on its meaning and how it applies to your life.

3. **Reflect on the Devotional**: Read the devotional message carefully. Consider how the insights and lessons shared can impact your faith journey. Allow the words to inspire and encourage you.

4. **Answer the Reflection Question**: Spend a few minutes contemplating the reflection question. You may want to write your thoughts in a journal. This exercise will help you internalize the message and apply it to your daily life.

5. **Declare the Decree Statement**: Speak the decree statement out loud with conviction. This act of faith reinforces the message and empowers you to live out the principles shared.

6. **Pray**: End your devotional time with prayer. Thank God for His word, ask for His guidance, and pray for the strength to apply what you've learned.

7. **Meditate Throughout the Day**: Carry the day's scripture, message, and decree with you. Reflect on them during the day and let them guide your actions and decisions.

Remember:

- **Consistency is Key**: Aim to use this devotional every day. Consistency will help you build a strong habit of spending time with God and growing in your faith.

- **Share Your Journey**: Consider sharing your reflections and insights with a friend or small group. Discussing your journey can provide additional support and encouragement.

- **Revisit and Reflect**: At the end of the 31 days, take time to revisit your journal entries and reflections. Reflect on your growth and the victories you've experienced.

Be Encouraged:

Remember, this devotional is a tool to help you draw closer to God and walk in the victory He has promised you. As you journey through these 31 days, may your faith be strengthened, your hope renewed, and your spirit uplifted. Trust that with God, every day can be a day of victory.

Devotional Guide

31 DAY
DEVOTIONAL

Prophetess Tera Person

DAY 1

FIGHT FOR IT!

"With God, all things are possible."
— Matthew 19:26

Fight For It!

Any dream or desire that God has placed in your heart, you can have. God would not have placed it in your heart if you couldn't have it. But first, you must believe that you can have it, be willing to put in the work to get it, and FIGHT FOR IT! Don't let doubt, disbelief, discouragement, or procrastination rob you of the dreams God has set up for you to have. You can do it, you can have it, IT'S YOURS! --- Believe ---

Decree Statement

I decree and declare I will not let doubt, disbelief, discouragement, or procrastination rob me of my God-given dreams. I will put in the work, believe in the possibilities, and fight for what is mine. With God, all things are possible, and I will achieve what He has placed in my heart, in the mighty name of Jesus.

Reflection Questions
What is one dream or desire that God has placed in your heart that you are willing to fight for? What steps can you take today to move closer to that dream?

DAY 2

STAY FOCUSED

"I can do all things through Christ who strengthens me."
— Philippians 4:13

Stay Focused

As you proceed to accomplish your God-given dreams or goals, distractions are inevitable. The enemy will use distractions of all sorts to slow you down or detour you. At these times, it is more important than ever to STAY FOCUSED. Don't allow distractions to hinder, delay, or stop your progress. Remember, success is a continual process of progress.

Decree Statement

I decree and declare that I will not let distractions hinder, delay, or stop my progress. I will stay focused on my God-given dreams and goals, knowing that with Christ's strength, I can overcome any obstacle. Success is a continual process of progress, and I am committed to moving forward, in the mighty name of Jesus.

Reflection Questions

What are some common distractions that tend to divert your attention from your goals? How can you minimize or eliminate these distractions to stay focused on your God-given dreams?

DAY 3

SPEAK VICTORY

"A man's stomach shall be satisfied from the fruit of his mouth; from the produce of his lips, he shall be filled. Death and life are in the power of the tongue, and those who love it will eat its fruit." — Proverbs 18:20-21

Speak Victory

Words have power. You cannot speak defeat and expect to have victory. You must speak healing, deliverance, restoration, joy, peace, success, great prosperity, and all these kinds of things because they will certainly render results. Be sure not to speak words that will bring you defeat. The word of God is true. So, SPEAK VICTORY.

Decree Statement
I decree and declare that I will speak words of healing, deliverance, restoration, joy, peace, success, and great prosperity. I reject words of defeat and embrace the power of positive, victorious declarations.

With my words, I will create the life of victory that God has promised me, in the mighty name of Jesus.

Reflection Questions

What negative words or phrases do you find yourself speaking that may be hindering your progress? How can you replace them with words of victory and positivity?

"If you can believe, all things are possible to him who believes." — Mark 9:23

Believe

Half of the battle is actually believing you can do what God said you can do and that you can have what He said you can have. God's desires for you are good, and He has equipped you with everything you need to reach your destiny. Believe it, and you shall achieve it.

Decree Statement

I decree and declare that I will believe in the promises and plans that God has for me. I am equipped with everything I need to reach my destiny. With faith and belief, I know that all things are possible through Him, in the mighty name of Jesus.

Reflection Questions

What is one promise or goal from God that you have struggled to believe fully? How can you strengthen your belief and trust in God's promises today?

DAY 5

PRAYER CHANGES EVERYTHING!

"Therefore I say to you, whatever things you ask when you pray, believe that you receive them, and you will have them."
— Mark 11:24

Prayer Changes Everything

There is power in prayer, just as there is power in the name of Jesus. The word of God is true; it will not return to Him void (Isaiah 55:11). So when you pray, expect to see God move on your behalf. Expect His blessings. Prayer is inviting God into your situation to intervene on your behalf. More importantly, prayer is the key to opening the door that Faith unlocks. Nothing is too hard for God. When you pray, believe that you have already received what you have petitioned for, and you will have exactly what you have prayed for.

Decree Statement

I decree and declare that I will bring my needs and desires to God in prayer, believing that He will act on my behalf. I trust in the power of prayer and the truth of God's word. With faith, I will receive what I have prayed for and witness God's blessings in my life, in the mighty name of Jesus.

Reflection Questions

What specific situation in your life do you need to bring to God in prayer? How can you deepen your faith and trust that God will move on your behalf?

DAY 6

SEEK GOD FIRST

"But seek first the kingdom of God and His righteousness, and all these things will be added to you." — Matthew 6:33

Seek God First

In the world we live in today, there are always people, places, things, and concepts competing for our attention. With that being said, we must not lose sight of who and what is most important: our Lord and Savior Jesus and the kingdom of God. Nothing and no one can give us eternity as a guarantee but Christ Jesus. One may lose eternity seeking things, and another will gain everything seeking Christ. Nothing is more important than eternity.

Decree Statement

I decree and declare I will seek first the kingdom of God and His righteousness. I will not let the distractions of this world take my focus away from what is most important: my relationship with Christ and the promise of eternity. By seeking God first, I trust that all other things will be added to me, in the mighty name of Jesus.

Reflection Questions
What are some distractions in your life that compete with your focus on God? How can you prioritize seeking God and His kingdom above all else?

DAY 7

STEADFAST AND
IMMOVABLE

"Therefore, my beloved brethren, be ye steadfast, unmoveable, always abounding in the work of the Lord, forasmuch as ye know that your labor is not in vain in the Lord." — 1 Corinthians 15:58

Steadfast and Immovable

Certain times in life we may require rest, and that's okay. But at all times in our life we are required to be steadfast and immovable when it comes to the word of God and the purpose of God. Don't give the enemy any place in your life. Remember, if we are not gaining new territory spiritually or otherwise, we may be losing it and not even realize it. So be on guard, watching, waiting, preparing, and remaining steadfast and immovable because sometimes victory is lost due to a lack of endurance. Stand, remain. Hold fast to your faith. This battle is not yours, and your victory is attached to you being immovable.

Decree Statement

I decree and declare I will be steadfast and immovable in my faith and the work of the Lord. I will not give the enemy any place in my life. I will stand firm, knowing that my labor in the Lord is not in vain. My victory is assured as I remain unwavering in my faith and purpose, in the mighty name of Jesus.

Reflection Questions

In what areas of your spiritual life do you need to be more steadfast and immovable? How can you ensure that you are always abounding in the work of the Lord?

DAY 8

DECREE A THING

"Thou shalt also decree a thing, and it shall be established
unto thee; and the light shall shine upon thy ways."
— Job 22:28

Decree A Thing

When you decree and declare a thing, you are putting spiritual
principles into action. You are exercising your God-given dominion,
power, and authority. As you make plans for your life and set goals,
start decreeing and declaring health, favor, blessings, success,
protection, prosperity, and all other things that are good over your life
and future. The more you speak it and seek it, the more you shall
see and receive the things you have decreed.

Decree Statement

I decree and declare I will exercise my God-given dominion, power,
and authority by speaking life, health, favor, blessings, success,
protection, and prosperity over my life. I trust that as I decree and

declare these things, they will be established, and I will see and receive God's promises, in the mighty name of Jesus.

Reflection Questions
What positive decrees and declarations can you start making over your life today? How can these decrees align with God's promises for you?

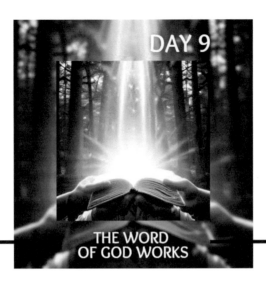

DAY 9

THE WORD OF GOD WORKS

"So shall My word be that goes forth from My mouth; it shall not return to Me void, but it shall accomplish what I please, and it shall prosper in the thing for which I sent it."
— Isaiah 55:11

The Word of God Works!

There are few things in the world that are guaranteed. Here are a few: taxes, death, and the word of God. The word will accomplish what it is sent out to do. Say, "No weapon formed against me shall prosper" (Isaiah 54:17); "I am more than a conqueror" (Romans 8:37); "I am the lender and not the borrower, God has made me the head and not the tail, above only and not beneath" (Deuteronomy 28:12-13); "I am blessed to be a blessing" (Genesis 12:2). Search the word for whatever you may need or desire and begin speaking it. The word of God will do exactly what it says it will do when you speak it and have faith.

Decree Statement

I decree and declare that the word of God will accomplish what it is sent out to do in my life. I will speak His promises over my life, trusting that no weapon formed against me shall prosper, I am more than a conqueror, I am the head and not the tail, and I am blessed to be a blessing. God's word will prosper in my life as I speak it with faith, in the mighty name of Jesus.

Reflection Questions

What specific promises from God's word can you begin speaking over your life today? How have you seen the word of God work in your life before?

DAY 10

FAITH FOR IT

"For we walk by faith, not by sight."
— 2 Corinthians 5:7

Faith For It

We operate on a system that the world does not. The kingdom of God's principles and laws are not the same as the world system. The world says believe it when you see it. The word says believe it and you will see it. When we operate this way, we are operating according to the principles in the kingdom of God. Faith brings forth the things from the spiritual realm that are invisible and makes them manifest in the physical form that others would call impossible. But you must have faith for it!

Decree Statement

I decree and declare I will walk by faith and not by sight. I will believe in God's promises even before I see them manifest. My faith will bring forth the invisible things from the spiritual realm and make them visible in my life. I trust in the principles of the kingdom of God and will operate by faith, in the mighty name of Jesus.

Reflection Questions

In what areas of your life do you need to exercise more faith? How can you strengthen your faith to believe in the unseen promises of God?

DAY 11

SPEAK THE NAME

"Therefore, God also has highly exalted Him and given Him the name which is above every name, that at the name of Jesus every knee should bow, of those in heaven, and of those on earth, and of those under the earth, and that every tongue should confess that Jesus Christ is Lord, to the glory of God the Father."
— Philippians 2:9-11

Speak The Name

The power that the name of Jesus carries is incomprehensible. It is incomparable, unequivocal, and no name in heaven, earth, or the universe holds more power and authority than the name of Jesus Christ. Unseen realms are subject to it; what seems impossible, the name of Jesus moves it. So speak the name of Jesus and witness the amazing power it exhibits. He is Lord of Lords and King of Kings, rescuer, deliverer, provider, and so much more. Everything changes when we speak the name of Jesus.

Decree Statement

I decree and declare I will speak the name of Jesus over every situation in my life. I acknowledge the unmatched power and authority of His name. As I speak the name of Jesus, I believe that every knee shall bow and every tongue shall confess that He is Lord. I will witness the miraculous power of Jesus in my life, in the mighty name of Jesus.

Reflection Questions

How have you experienced the power of Jesus' name in your life? In what situations do you need to speak His name to witness a change?

DAY 12

HE IS!

"For the kingdom of God is not in word but in power."
— 1 Corinthians 4:20

He Is!

He is God the Father, God the Son, God the Holy Spirit, and they are ONE. God is who is, who was, and is to come, the Almighty (Revelation 1:8). He is the Prince of Peace and Wonderful Counselor (Isaiah 9:6). He is the giver of every perfect gift (James 1:17). He is the author and finisher of our faith (Hebrews 12:2). He is Alpha and Omega, Beginning and the End (Revelation 1:8). And He is worthy to be praised!

Decree Statement

I decree and declare that I recognize and honor God for who He is: the Almighty, the Prince of Peace, the Wonderful Counselor, the giver of every perfect gift, the author and finisher of my faith, the Alpha and Omega. I praise Him for His power and majesty, knowing

24

that He is worthy of all my worship and adoration, in the mighty name of Jesus.

Reflection Questions

Which attribute of God mentioned above resonates most with you today? How can acknowledging this aspect of God deepen your faith and trust in Him?

DAY 13

MORE THAN
A CONQUEROR

"Greater is He that is in you than he that is in the world."
— 1 John 4:4

More Than A Conqueror

The word of God is designed to guide, direct, equip, and produce positive results in our lives. Here is why that is true: In the beginning was the WORD, the word was with God, and the word was God (John 1:1). Because He lives in us once we are born again, we have overcoming power. With that power, and through that power, we are more than conquerors through Christ who loved us (Romans 8:37). More than means above and beyond things and circumstances. Every word from God is true; we just have to believe.

Decree Statement

I decree and declare that I am more than a conqueror through Christ who loves me. I embrace the overcoming power that resides within me, knowing that every word from God is true. I will rise above and beyond all things and circumstances, believing in the power of God's word, in the mighty name of Jesus.

Reflection Questions

In what areas of your life do you need to embrace the truth that you are more than a conqueror? How can you tap into the overcoming power that resides within you through Christ?

DAY 14

IT'S WORKING
FOR YOUR GOOD

"And we know that all things work together for good to those who love God, to those who are called according to His purpose." — Romans 8:28

It's Working For Your Good

Everything that happens in life doesn't always seem to make sense. Sometimes, situations become overwhelming, and the future looks bleak. But rest assured that this too shall pass. Weeping may endure for a night, but hallelujah, joy comes in the morning. What the enemy meant for evil, God will turn it around and make it work for good (Genesis 50:20). We serve a God who is all-knowing, and nothing catches Him by surprise. With that being said, have confidence in His power and purpose. It's working for our good.

Decree Statement

I decree and declare that all things are working together for my good because I love God and am called according to His purpose. Even in difficult times, I trust in His power and purpose, knowing that He will turn every situation around for my benefit, in the mighty name of Jesus.

Reflection Questions

Can you think of a time when a difficult situation ultimately worked out for your good? How can remembering this help you trust God's purpose in your current circumstances?

DAY 15

DO YOU
RECEIVE IT?

"Now to Him who is able to do exceedingly abundantly above all that we ask or think, according to the power that works in us, to Him be glory in the church by Christ Jesus to all generations, forever and ever. Amen."
— Ephesians 3:20-21

Do You Receive It?

Take time to think about all the goodness of God. His magnificence, His majesty, His mercy, His grace, His love, His favor, His power, His healing, His deliverance, His knowledge, His wisdom, all of His blessings, His protection, His direction, His correction ("Whom the Lord loves He corrects" - Proverbs 3:12), His goodness, His miraculous works, His faithfulness, His answers to prayers, His promises that He is faithful to keep, His profound evidence of His existence, and so much more. Our Lord and Savior Jesus Christ has given us access to this and all the more; we just have to receive it.

Decree Statement

I decree and declare that I receive all the goodness of God in my life. I acknowledge His magnificence, mercy, grace, love, favor, power, healing, deliverance, wisdom, and countless blessings. I open my heart to receive even more, trusting in His faithfulness and miraculous works, in the mighty name of Jesus.

Reflection Questions

Reflect on the various attributes and blessings of God listed above. Which of these have you experienced in your life recently? How can you open your heart to receive more of God's goodness?

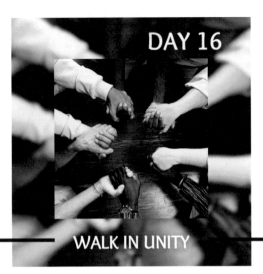

DAY 16

WALK IN UNITY

track

"I do not pray for these alone, but also for those who will believe in Me through their word; that they all may be one, as You, Father, are in Me, and I in You; that they also may be one in Us." — John 17:20-21

Walk In Unity

As part of the body of Christ, it is important for us to be unified in our faith with Christ as the head of the body. We should exhibit Godly love to one another and to others. There is power in unity with Christ and each other that removes unseen barriers and releases a multitude of blessings that have been hindered or delayed. We are to pray for one another, exhort and uplift one another. All of this comes when we are in unity with Christ, which pleases our Father God.

Decree Statement

I decree and declare that I will walk in unity with my brothers and sisters in Christ. I will demonstrate Godly love, pray for others, and uplift those around me. I embrace the power of unity, knowing that it removes barriers and releases blessings. Through unity with Christ, we become one body, pleasing to our Father God, in the mighty name of Jesus.

Reflection Questions

How can you foster greater unity within your church or community? In what ways can you demonstrate Godly love and support to others to build a stronger bond of unity?

DAY 17

POSITION YOURSELF

"I am the vine, you are the branches. He who abides in Me, and I in him bears much fruit; for without Me you can do nothing." — John 15:5 (Read John 15:1-8)

Position Yourself

For us to reach our full potential or fulfill our God-given purpose, we have to be in position. This means if you're called to start a ministry, business, write a book, open a school, a bank for the kingdom, or anything else, we must acquire the knowledge needed. We must also develop the gift or talent by using it, practicing it, or polishing it, gaining new skills to complement the gift or talent, building relationships that nurture the calling or purpose, etc. More importantly, we are to be obedient to the voice of God, the will of God, and the word of God. Our Heavenly Father has a purpose for each one of us that becomes clearer as we grow in Him, which opens doors of perfect opportunity when we position ourselves.

Decree Statement

I decree and declare that I will position myself to fulfill God's purpose in my life. I will acquire the necessary knowledge, develop my gifts and talents, and build relationships that support my calling. Above all, I will remain obedient to the voice, will, and word of God, knowing that through Him, I will bear much fruit, in the mighty name of Jesus.

Reflection Questions

What steps do you need to take to better position yourself for the purpose God has for you? How can you develop your gifts and talents to align with His calling?

DAY 18

PRAISE HIM IN ADVANCE

"But You are holy, enthroned in the praises of Israel."
— Psalm 22:3

Praise Him in Advance

Something wonderful takes place when we are in times of praise. A loud shout of "Thank you Jesus! Hallelujah!" from a believer's heart gets God's attention. Praying brings us into the presence of God, but praising brings God into our presence. When the presence of the Lord shows up where you are, His peace, joy, love, healing, and deliverance power show up as well. The Bible says He inhabits the praise of His people. So right now, if you want things to shift, if you need a breakthrough, start praising. Praise Him as if you already have it and glorify Him for it before you see it. That kind of praise reveals faith, and He will show up right in the middle of your praise, even when you don't see it. Believe it and it shall be done.

Decree Statement

I decree and declare that I will praise God in advance for the breakthroughs, blessings, and answers I am believing for. I will lift my voice in faith, knowing that He inhabits the praises of His people. I trust that God will show up in my praise, bringing His peace, joy, love, healing, and deliverance, in the mighty name of Jesus.

Reflection Questions

What are you believing God for that you can start praising Him for in advance? How can you incorporate more praise into your daily life to invite God's presence and power?

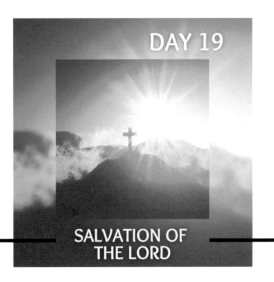

SALVATION OF
THE LORD

"He shall call upon Me, and I will answer him; I will be with him in trouble. I will deliver him and honor him. With long life I will satisfy him and show him My salvation."
— Psalm 91:15-16

The Lord Is Your Salvation

The word salvation means "preservation or deliverance from harm, ruin, or loss." It also means "a state of being saved or protected from harm or a dire situation." That is the definition in the dictionary. However, the biblical meaning of salvation is the redemptive power of Jesus Christ that has saved us from the consequences of sin as well as eternal death and separation from God. What a mighty God we serve! Salvation is one of the most beautiful opportunities we have access to through Christ and is a gift from God. However, this gift should not be taken for granted but rather cherished and appreciated. Salvation is one of God's greatest examples of love. That is why Jesus died on the cross. The Lord is our salvation!

Decree Statement

I decree and declare that I will cherish and appreciate the gift of salvation that God has given me through Jesus Christ. I recognize the redemptive power of Jesus that has saved me from sin and eternal separation from God. I will live my life in gratitude, honoring the Lord for His great love and salvation, in the mighty name of Jesus.

Reflection Questions

How has the gift of salvation impacted your life personally? In what ways can you show your appreciation for this gift from God?

THE GIVER OF
EVERY PERFECT GIFT

"A man's gift makes room for him and brings him
before great men." — Proverbs 18:16

The Giver of Every Perfect Gift

Our Heavenly Father is gracious with what He has instilled in us and
upon us. He has created no one without a gift. Some have more gifts
than others, but everyone has a gift. Your gift is the thing or things
you do the best with the least amount of effort. That is your gift. It is
to be used and developed to increase its value and prominence.
More than that, it is to be used to glorify God. He has equipped us
with everything we need to overcome and come out in victory. Too
often we look in the wrong places for what God has placed inside of
us. Your gift has great value, and when you invest in it, you'll reap a
profitable return.

Decree Statement

I decree and declare that I will recognize and develop the gifts God has placed inside of me. I will use my gifts to glorify Him, knowing that He has equipped me with everything I need to overcome and achieve victory. I will invest in my gifts and trust that they will make room for me and bring me before great men, in the mighty name of Jesus.

Reflection Questions

What gifts has God placed inside of you that you can develop and use to glorify Him? How can you invest in these gifts to bring them to their full potential?

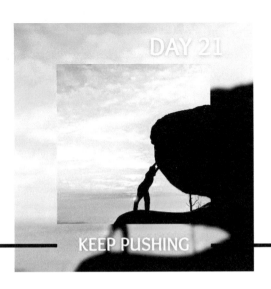

"Being confident of this very thing, that He who has begun a good work in you will complete it until the day of Jesus Christ." — Philippians 1:6

Keep Pushing

A person's failures in life don't determine who they are nearly as much as how they get back up. If someone has failed nine times and got up ten, their success will be determined by the 10th time they got up and how they stood. Sometimes we have to learn what it is to fail to be able to succeed. No successful person has achieved success without any losses or failures along the way. The difference between those who lose and those who win is the determination to get back up again. Thomas Edison had 999 failed attempts prior to successfully creating the light bulb. Yet, it was his 1,000th attempt that produced the light bulb. So keep pushing... get back up again. Your next try may very well be the awaited outcome you so very much desire.

Decree Statement

I decree and declare that I will keep pushing forward, regardless of setbacks and failures. I will rise each time I fall, confident that God, who began a good work in me, will complete it. I trust that my determination and perseverance will lead to the success and outcomes I desire, in the mighty name of Jesus.

Reflection Questions

What setbacks have you faced recently that you need to overcome? How can you develop the determination to keep pushing and trying again?

DAY 22

STANDING ON YOUR FAITH

"But without faith it is impossible to please Him, for he who comes to God must believe that He is, and that He is a rewarder of those who diligently seek Him." — Hebrews 11:6

"For with God nothing will be impossible." — Luke 1:37

Standing On Your Faith

One of the things that God requires of His children is faith. The scripture says, "But without faith it is impossible to please Him, for he who comes to God must believe that He is, and that He is a rewarder of those who diligently seek Him" (Hebrews 11:6). God keeps His promises and performs according to His word. Anything He has told you will come to pass. It doesn't matter what things may look like; your heavenly Father has miracle-working power and He is always pleased to bless His children. So stand on your faith; if God said it, He will do it.

Decree Statement

I decree and declare that I will stand on my faith, trusting in God's promises and His miracle-working power. I believe that with God, nothing is impossible. I will diligently seek Him, knowing that He is pleased to bless His children and fulfill His word, in the mighty name of Jesus.

Reflection Questions

What promises from God are you standing on in faith today? How can you strengthen your faith to trust in God's miracle-working power?

DAY 23

TRY AGAIN!

"Thanks be to God who gives us the victory through Christ Jesus." — 1 Corinthians 15:57

Try Again!

It's okay to try and fail. Trying and not succeeding does not make us a failure, just as running a race and not winning doesn't make you a loser. The concept of falling is nowhere near as important as how we get back up. Our greatest victories are revealed through the strength of our perseverance and the essence of our determination. So sometimes we may not be successful at an idea, task, or God-given dream, but that doesn't mean we stop there. All that means is that we take what we have learned and try again!

Decree Statement

I decree and declare that I will not be discouraged by failure but will take the lessons learned and try again. I trust that God, who began a good work in me, is faithful to complete it. I will persevere with determination, knowing that my greatest victories are yet to come, in the mighty name of Jesus.

Reflection Questions
What lessons have you learned from past attempts that didn't succeed? How can you apply those lessons and try again with renewed determination?

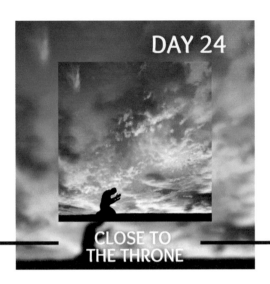

DAY 24

CLOSE TO
THE THRONE

"Set your mind on things above, not on things on the earth."
— Colossians 3:2

Close to The Throne

There are times in our lives where we need to stay much closer to the throne of God than we have before. Staying close to the throne of God provides us with encounters with the Holy Spirit that otherwise may not take place with distance between you and your heavenly Father. You will receive instruction, information, and knowledge with revelation. More importantly, you will gain intimacy with God that is imperative to building a bond with Him as well as strategies to bring you in and out in victory now and always. The closer we stay to the throne, the easier it is to recognize the enemy and stop him while he is still plotting.

Decree Statement

I decree and declare that I will stay close to the throne of God, seeking His presence and guidance daily. I will set my mind on things above and draw near to my heavenly Father. Through this closeness, I will receive revelation, build intimacy with God, and gain victory over the enemy, in the mighty name of Jesus.

Reflection Questions

In what ways can you draw closer to the throne of God in your daily life? How can staying close to God help you recognize and thwart the enemy's plans?

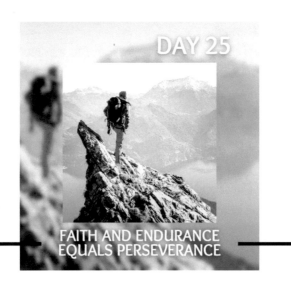

FAITH AND ENDURANCE
EQUALS PERSEVERANCE

"But he who endures to the end shall be saved."
— Matthew 24:13

Faith and Endurance Equals Perseverance

No one is off limits to trials, tribulations, or the testing of their faith. In fact, the Bible tells us to expect these things and count it all joy. Here's what James 1:2-4 says: "My brethren, count it all joy when you fall into various trials, knowing that the testing of your faith produces patience. But let patience have its perfect work, that you may be perfect and complete, lacking nothing." Our character is built when we are faced with challenges, and our faith grows with each battle we endure and come out victorious. Even when it doesn't turn out the way we would have it, we can rest assured that our Savior Jesus is in every battle with us, leading and guiding us. We just have to follow His lead, have faith, endure, and persevere.

Decree Statement

I decree and declare that I will face my trials and tribulations with joy, knowing that they test and strengthen my faith. I will have patience, endure, and persevere, trusting that Jesus is with me in every battle. My faith and endurance will lead me to victory and spiritual completeness, in the mighty name of Jesus.

Reflection Questions

What trials or challenges are you currently facing that are testing your faith? How can you rely on your faith and endurance to persevere through these difficulties?

GET THE JOB DONE!

" I can do ALL things through Christ who strengthens me."
— Philippians 4:13

Get The Job Done!

God has equipped each one of us with everything we need to complete our God-given assignments and fulfill His purpose and destiny for our lives. Nevertheless, many times believers get distracted and discouraged, causing them to abort the mission and leave their assignments incomplete. But even in those times, God is so very gracious that He has mercy on us and gives us another chance. If you are still here and reading this right now, that means God still has a purpose for you and is giving you an opportunity to get the job done!

Decree Statement

I decree and declare that I will focus on completing the assignments and purposes God has placed in my life. I trust that He who began a good work in me will complete it. I will not be discouraged or distracted but will push forward with the confidence that God has equipped me to get the job done, in the mighty name of Jesus.

Reflection Questions

What assignments or purposes has God placed in your life that you may have left incomplete? How can you refocus and take action to complete these tasks with the confidence that God will help you?

DAY 27

GRACE AND FAVOR

"For by grace you have been saved through faith, and that not of yourselves; it is the gift of God." — Ephesians 2:8

Grace and Favor

It is very difficult to think about the goodness of God without acknowledging the grace and favor He has bestowed upon us. There have been several times in believers' lives in which they can recall moments that it was nothing but the grace of God that caused them to live, survive, and thrive. In the same way, there have been times where God has given us unprecedented favor—the kind of favor that you know can only come from our Heavenly Father.

Decree Statement

I decree and declare that I will recognize and appreciate the grace and favor that God has bestowed upon my life. I am grateful for the moments when His grace has sustained me and His favor has opened doors. I will live with a heart full of gratitude, acknowledging God's goodness every day, in the mighty name of Jesus.

Reflection Questions

Can you recall specific instances in your life where you experienced God's grace and favor? How can reflecting on these moments strengthen your faith and gratitude?

DAY 28

HE IS
COMING SOON

"And behold, I am coming quickly, and My reward is with Me, to give to every one according to his work."
— Revelation 22:12

He Is Coming Soon

REJOICE! Our Lord and Savior is soon to return. He has promised us that He has gone to prepare a place for us, and as He promised, He will be returning (John 14:1-6). That is when those who have kept His commandments shall receive their reward of eternal life (Revelation 21:3-7; Matthew 25:23). Again, I say, REJOICE! Everything Jesus promised we shall receive. So, continue to fight the good fight of FAITH and do not grow weary in well-doing, for we shall reap if we do not faint (Galatians 6:9).

Decree Statement

I decree and declare that I will rejoice in the promise of Jesus' soon return. I will remain steadfast in my faith, keeping His

56

commandments, and continuing to do well. I trust in His promise that He is coming quickly, and His reward is with Him to give to everyone according to their work, in the mighty name of Jesus.

Reflection Questions

How does the promise of Jesus' return impact your daily life and faith? What steps can you take to remain steadfast in your faith and well-doing as you await His return?

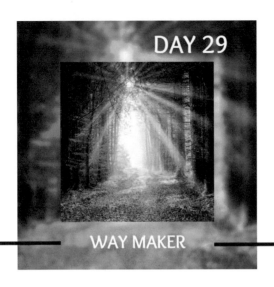

DAY 29

WAY MAKER

"For with God nothing will be impossible."
— Luke 1:37

Way Maker

We serve a faithful and wonderful God. The God who shut the lions' mouths, stopped three young men from being burned alive even after they were in the furnace, and the One who split the Red Sea so His chosen people could travel on dry land. He is the God who is our healer, deliverer, and defender. The one true God, Jehovah Jireh, our provider, and Jehovah Nissi, our prince of peace. The God who performs miracles, who is almighty, all-powerful, supreme, and none is above Him nor can compare. He is a Way Maker.

Decree Statement

I decree and declare that I serve a faithful and wonderful God who is my Way Maker. I trust in His power and might, knowing that with God, nothing is impossible. I will remember His past miracles and trust Him to make a way for me in every situation, in the mighty name of Jesus.

Reflection Questions

Can you recall a time when God made a way for you when it seemed impossible? How does remembering His past faithfulness help you trust Him for your current needs?

DAY 30

ASK AND YOU
SHALL RECEIVE

"Ask, and it will be given to you; seek, and you will find; knock, and it will be opened to you." — Matthew 7:7

"Let us therefore come boldly to the throne of grace, that we may obtain mercy and find grace to help in time of need." — Hebrews 4:16

Ask and You Shall Receive

The Bible tells us in Hebrews 4:16, "Let us come boldly to the throne of grace that we may obtain mercy and find grace in time of need." The throne of God is always open to us. We are to take our needs, wants, worries, or concerns to the throne of God and leave them there. We are to pray and believe, ask and expect to receive. Our Heavenly Father has an unlimited amount of resources and He is always looking for ways to bless us. Our duty is to pray, petition, decree, and declare, have faith, and believe. Then we will see God's miracle-working power.

Decree Statement

I decree and declare that I will come boldly to the throne of grace with my needs, wants, and concerns. I will pray, petition, decree, and declare with faith, believing that God will answer and provide. I trust in His unlimited resources and His desire to bless me, in the mighty name of Jesus.

Reflection Questions

What needs, desires, or concerns do you need to bring boldly before the throne of God? How can you strengthen your faith to believe and expect to receive His blessings?

DAY 31

VICTORY IS YOURS!

"Yet in all these things we are more than conquerors through Him who loved us." — Romans 8:37

"No weapon formed against you shall prosper." — Isaiah 54:17

"Behold, I give you the authority to trample on serpents and scorpions, and over all the power of the enemy, and nothing shall by any means hurt you." — Luke 10:19

"Now thanks be to God who always leads us in triumph in Christ." — 2 Corinthians 2:14

Victory Is Yours!

The Bible is very clear about all of our victories and how to achieve them. Through Christ, we have strength, we are more than conquerors, and no weapon formed against us shall prosper. God has given us power and authority over the devil and all his works.

Victory is ours in every area! Thanks be to God, who always causes us to triumph.

Decree Statement

I decree and declare that victory is mine in every area of my life. Through Christ, who strengthens me, I am more than a conqueror. No weapon formed against me shall prosper. I have power and authority over all the works of the enemy. Thanks be to God who always causes me to triumph, in the mighty name of Jesus.

Reflection Questions

In what areas of your life do you need to claim victory today? How can you remind yourself daily of the power and authority you have in Christ to overcome any challenge?

WE STAND ON

Genesis 12:2-3

"I will make you a great nation; I will bless you and make your name great; and you shall be a blessing. I will bless those who bless you, and I will curse him who curses you; and in you, all the families of the earth shall be blessed."

Numbers 6:22-27

"And the LORD spoke to Moses, saying: 'Speak to Aaron and his sons, saying, "This is the way you shall bless the children of Israel. Say to them: 'The LORD bless you and keep you; the LORD make His face shine upon you, and be gracious to you; the LORD lift up His countenance upon you, and give you peace. 'So they shall put My name on the children of Israel, and I will bless them.'"

Deuteronomy 8:6-10, 18

"Therefore you shall keep the commandments of the LORD your God, to walk in His ways and to fear Him. For the LORD your God is bringing you into a good land, a land of brooks of water, of fountains

64

and springs, that flow out of valleys and hills; a land of wheat and barley, of vines and fig trees and pomegranates, a land of olive oil and honey; a land in which you will eat bread without scarcity, in which you will lack nothing; a land whose stones are iron and out of whose hills you can dig copper. When you have eaten and are full, then you shall bless the LORD your God for the good land which He has given you.

18: "And you shall remember the LORD your God, for it is He who gives you power to get wealth, that He may establish His covenant which He swore to your fathers, as it is this day."

Deuteronomy 28:12-13
"The LORD will open to you His good treasure, the heavens, to give the rain to your land in its season, and to bless all the work of your hand. You shall lend to many nations, but you shall not borrow. And the LORD will make you the head and not the tail; you shall be above only, and not be beneath, if you heed the commandments of the LORD your God, which I command you today, and are careful to observe them."

No weapon formed against us will prosper. We are more than conquerors. As for me and my house, we will serve the Lord. I can do all things through Christ who strengthens me. We are blessed to be a blessing. Thanks be to God, who always causes us to triumph. We live a long, lavish, prosperous life in divine health, fulfilling our God-given purpose and destiny with our names written in the book of life generationally. When it's all said and done, we will hear, "Well done, good and faithful servant." In the Mighty Name of Jesus, we decree and declare it done.

DECREE!

I increase, We increase in:

Healing, Forgiveness, Freedom, Health, Safety, Protection, Favor, Blessings, Houses, Land, Silver, Gold, Love, Joy, Peace, Success, Power and Authority, Great Prosperity, Knowledge, Wisdom, Understanding, Faith, Righteousness, Holiness, Unity, Peace, Discernment, Revelation, Obedience, and Discipline.

This is for us, our family, friends, and ministries. And when we do, we will not forget the Lord, our God. We will serve Him, worship Him, and obey Him all the days of our lives. We decree it and declare it done, in the mighty name of Jesus.

66

Made in the USA
Columbia, SC
22 August 2024

40828902R00042